D0831013

First published in Great Britain in 1996 by Brockhampton Press,
a member of the Hodder Headline Group,
20 Bloomsbury Street, London WC1B 3QA.

This series of little gift books was made by Frances Banfield, Kate Brown, Laurel Clark, Penny Clarke, Clive Collins, Melanie Cumming, Nick Diggory, Deborah Gill, David Goodman, Douglas Hall, Maureen Hill, Nick Hutchison, John Hybert, Kate Hybert, Douglas Ingram, Simon London, Patrick McCreeth, Morse Modaberi, Tara Neill, Anne Newman, Grant Oliver, Michelle Rogers, Nigel Soper, Karen Sullivan and Nick Wells.

ISBN 1 86019 464 8
A copy of the CIP data is available from the
British Library upon request.

Produced for Brockhampton Press by Flame Tree Publishing,
part of The Foundry Creative Media Company Limited,
The Long House, Antrobus Road, Chiswick W4 5HY.

Printed and bound in Italy by L.E.G.O. Spa.

The Funny Book of COMPUTERS

Words selected by
Bob Hale

Cartoons by
Nick Diggory

If Adam and Eve had an Apple, why did they have so much trouble accessing God's instructions?

Doctor: I fed all your symptoms into the computer, Mrs Jones, and it died.

If operating systems were beer:

Mac Beer: At first, came only in a sixteen-ounce can, but now comes in a thirty-two-ounce can. Considered by many to be a 'light' beer. All the cans look identical. When you take one from the fridge, it opens itself. The ingredients list is not on the can. If you call to ask about the ingredients, you are told that you 'don't need to know'. A notice on the side reminds you to drag your empties to the trash can.

"THE ANTI-GLARE SCREEN'S A GREAT IDEA MARILYN, BUT SHOULDN'T IT GO ON THE COMPUTER?"

The computer fanatic knows that computers are infallible ... it is the Human Factor that messes things up.

Police take away a felon from the office where he worked. One bystander to another: 'They've arrested him for the computer fraud and the computer as an accessory.'

Computer error: the fifth pestilence.

A computer is only as inept as the fellow at the keyboard.

If a well-known computer company made cars:

1. We have released a new car but users will have to wait for a later date for the car's engine to be completed.
2. ONLY applies to this type of car since software for cars has been engineered to be backward compatible with models from prior years.
3. These cars would also die for no apparent reason while other cars would continue to run, only when asked what the problem was, you would be informed only that it 'Unexpectedly Quit'.
4. These cars STILL only allow one individual to be present in the car at a time, although promises have been made to make a multiple passenger vehicle in the future.

5 This company would offer a car that boasted being much more reliable and at least twice as fast as software for cars although none of these factors could be proven in Motor Trend tests.

6 Warning lights are not included in these cars since the users would not understand them anyway.

7 This company claims that their automobile has always had features that the software company has just now announced, aside from not being able to house more than one passenger or allow user access to the engine.

Virtual shopping is great ... browsing through the aisles ... finding virtually every product ... I wonder if they'll accept a virtual cheque?

Compuserve advertising slogan

TECHNO
DWEEB

If operating systems were beer:

DOS Beer: Requires you to use your own can opener, and requires you to read the directions carefully before opening the can. Originally only came in an eight-ounce can, but now comes in a sixteen-ounce can. However, the can is divided into eight compartments of two ounces each, which have to be accessed separately. Soon to be discontinued, although a lot of people are going to keep drinking it after it's no longer available.

Everything that can be invented has been invented.

Charles H. Duell,

Commissioner, US Office of Patents, 1899

Signs that you haven't quite caught up with technology:

1 You think Megabyte is a remake of Jaws.
2 You can add in your head easier and faster than you can open up the calculator on the computer.
3 You think that the World Wide Web is a plot line from Spiderman.
4 You think the Internet is a fisheries dispute in Canada.
5 When someone says they are a Mac person you automatically think that they are into sexual perversion.
6 You think Bill Gates owns a rubber factory in Denver.
7 You think that reformatting your drive is a golf lesson.
8 When someone says 'scuzzy drive' you automatically think of East Colfax.
9 When someone tries to sell you a computer you look at the price not the speed.
10 You thought lap tops were for sitting in.

"....AND IF YOU DON'T STOP PESTERING DADDY FOR A VIRTUAL REALITY HEADSET, DADDY'S GOING TO GIVE YOU A VIRTUAL REALITY THICK EAR!"

If operating systems were beer:

Windows 3.1 Beer: The world's most popular. Comes in a sixteen-ounce can that looks a lot like Mac Beer's. Requires that you already own a DOS beer. Claims that it allows you to drink several DOS Beers simultaneously, but in reality you can only drink a few of them, very slowly, especially slowly if you are drinking the Windows Beer at the same time. Sometimes, for no apparent reason, a can of Windows Beer will explode when you open it.

Computers come in two varieties:
the prototype and the obsolete.

Technology is a queer thing.
It brings you great gifts with one hand,
and it stabs you in the back with the other.

C.P. Snow

MENU
FISH
CHIPS
MICROCHIPS

CRASH

"I SAID, IF YOU PRESS "ALT F1", I CAN TALK TO YOU OVER THE NETWORK!!!

Boss: Did you know that twenty per cent of all microfleems are subradiante?
Employee (to himself): Uh, oh. The boss has latched on to some obscure engineering fact ... this is going to be painful.
Boss: Just think of the implications. It means eight per cent of microfleems are not subradiante.
Employee (to himself): Maybe I can hide under the desk until this blows over ...
Boss: Don't you think it's fascinating? I mean, what with the implications and all ...
Employee: OK, OK, I acknowledge your incredible grasp of technology issues.
Boss (to himself): It almost makes me curious what a microfleem is ...

*Scott Adams, **Dilbert***

Abandon hope all yea who press ENTER here.

If operating systems were beer:

OS/2 Beer: Comes in a thirty-two-ounce can. Does allow you to drink several DOS Beers simultaneously. Allows you to drink Windows 3.1 Beer simultaneously too, but somewhat slower. Advertises that its cans won't explode when you open them, even if you shake them up. You never really see anyone drinking 0S/2 Beer, but the manufacturer (International Beer Manufacturing) claims that nine million six-packs have been sold.

Q: How many programmers does it take to change a light bulb?

A: None, that's a hardware problem.

"NUMBER 1-BOOT UP THE COMPUTER...."
INSTRUCTION MANUAL

"RAM! HA, WHAT A STUPID NAME FOR SOMETHING SO CLEVER!!"
RAM

Q: How many managers does it take to change a light bulb?

A: We've formed a task force to study the problem of why light bulbs burn out and to figure out what, exactly, we as supervisors can do to make the bulbs work smarter not harder.

Q: How many software testers does it take to change a light bulb?

A: We just noticed the room was dark; we don't actually fix light bulbs.

Q: How many software developers does it take to change a light bulb?

A: The light bulb works fine on the system in my office.

"YOU'D
HARD
CLEANED
CHECKED
OUT
YOU'RE
CLEAN
AGAIN."

RTED A VIRUS ONTO YOUR
E FROM SOME DODGY
SOFTWARE. BUT I'VE

TAP!
TAP!

TECHNICAL SUPPORT TEAM

Q: How many computer programmers does it take to change a lightbulb?

A: Eight. One to analyse the problem, one to write the program, one to understand and debug the program, one to carry out the instructions and four to write the documentation.

Seven years is two lifetimes in
the microcomputer industry.

John Sculley, ***Odyssey: Pepsi to Apple***

Dear Mr Jobs
I was doing a crossword puzzle and a clue was, 'As American as Apple –'. I thought the answer was computer, but my mom said 'pie'.

Letter to Steve Jobs (founder of Apple Computer Company), from a six-and-a-half-year-old boy

PAINT
MASTER

If operating systems were beer:

Windows 95 Beer: A lot of people have taste-tested it and claim it's wonderful. The can looks a lot like Mac Beer's can, but tastes more like Windows 3.1 Beer. It comes in thirty-two-ounce cans, but when you look inside, the cans have only sixteen ounces of beer in them. Most people will probably keep drinking Windows 3.1 Beer until their friends try Windows 95 Beer and say they like it. The ingredients list, when you look at the small print, has some of the same ingredients that come in DOS Beer, even though the manufacturer claims that this is an entirely new brew.

When I was a boy, an apple was something you brought the teacher. Today, you learn on an Apple or a Macintosh.

Ronald Reagan

"CAN I SEND THIS
BY E-MAIL
PLEASE?"

Employer: You should have been behind your computer this morning at nine sharp.
Late employee: Why, what happened?

Milton [Berle] says he has compiled the largest collection of humour material in the world: 6,000,000 jokes, thousands of radio and television scripts and vaudeville routines, all indexed on a computer.

*George Burns, **All My Best Friends***

Smith's Law of Computer Repair:
Access holes will be half an inch too small.
Corollary:
Holes that are the right size will be in the wrong place.

*Arthur Bloch, **Murphy's Law Complete***

Fifth Law of Unreliability:
To err is human, but to really foul
things up requires a computer.
Arthur Bloch, ***Murphy's Law Complete***

Computers can figure out all
kinds of problems, except the things
in the world that just don't add up.
James Magary

We used to have lots of questions to
which there were no answers. Now, with
the computer, there are lots of answers to
which we haven't thought up the questions.
Peter Ustinov

MOTHER BORED!

DAUGHTER BORED!!

If operating systems were beer:

Windows NT Beer: Comes in thirty-two-ounce cans, but you can only buy it by the truckload. This causes most people to have to go out and buy bigger refrigerators. The can looks just like Windows 95's Beer. Touted as an 'industrial strength' beer, and suggested only for use in bars.

A modern computer hovers between
the obsolescent and the non-existent.

Sydney Brenner

It's wonderful things they're doing now –
There's marriages by computer,
Just feed in her vital statistics,
And find the poor girl a suitor.

Raymond Howe, ***A Technological Age***

SMACK!

Any sufficiently advanced technology
is indistinguishable from magic.
Arthur C. Clarke, ***The Lost Worlds of 2001***

If operating systems were beer:
Unix Beer: Comes in several different brands, in cans ranging from eight ounces to sixty-four ounces. Drinkers of Unix Beer display fierce brand loyalty, even though they claim that all the different brands taste almost identical. Sometimes the pop-tops break off when you try to open them, so you have to have your own can opener around for those occasions, in which case you either need a complete set of instructions or a friend who has been drinking Unix Beer for several years.

Computers in the future may weigh no more than 1.5 tons.

***Popular Mechanics**, forecasting the relentless march of science, 1949*

I think there is a world market for maybe five computers.

Thomas Watson, chairman of IBM, 1943

I have travelled the length and breadth of this country and talked with the best people, and I can assure you that data processing is a fad that won't last out the year.

Business books editor at Prentice Hall, 1957

But what ... is it good for?

Engineer at the Advanced Computing Systems Division of IBM, 1968, commenting on the microchip

There is no reason anyone would want a computer in their home.

Ken Olson, president, chairman and founder of Digital Equipment Corporation, 1977

If operating systems were beer:

AmigaDOS Beer: The company has gone out of business, but their recipe has been picked up from some weird German company, so now this beer will be an import. The beer never really sold very well because the original manufacturers didn't understand marketing. Like Unix Beer, AmigaDOS Beer fans are an extremely loyal and loud group. It originally came in a sixteen-ounce can, but now comes in thirty-two-ounce cans, too. When this can was originally introduced, it appeared flashy and colourful, but the design hasn't changed much over the years, so it appears dated now. Critics of this beer claim that it is only meant for watching TV anyhow.

"I WAS JUST SHOWING GRANDAD MY LATEST GAME."
CYBORG MEGA DEATH!!

If PCs were cars:

1 A particular model of car wouldn't be available until after that year.

2 Every time they repainted the lines on the road, you'd have to buy a new engine for your car – unless your car was more than two years old; then you'd have to buy a new car.

3 Occasionally your car would just die for no apparent reason, while other cars would continue about their business.

4 You could only have one person at a time in your car, unless you have a WinCar95 or a CarNT, but then, you'd have to buy more seats and seatbelts.

5 Sun Motorsystems would make a car that was solar-powered, twice as reliable, five times as fast, but only ran on five per cent of the roads.

6 The oil, alternator, petrol and engine warning lights would be replaced with a single light that reads: 'General Car Fault, please restart'.

7 Apple could make a car that featured a low cost, yet very powerful V10 engine that was three times as reliable, four to five times faster, but the press would slam every new model no matter what the public's reaction was.

8 Each morning, you'd have to take your software steering wheel out to your car, install it using the software company's plug and play technology, but twenty per cent of the time your car would not recognize the steering wheel, and you'd have to reinstall it from scratch at the dealer. For some strange reason, this would not bother you.

The genius of modern technology is
making things to last fifty years and
then making them obsolete in three.

Anonymous

So we went to Atari and said, 'Hey, we've got this amazing thing, even built with some of your parts, and what do you think about funding us? Or we'll give it to you. We just want to do it. Pay our salary, we'll come work for you.' And they said, 'No.' So then we went to Hewlett-Packard, and they said, 'Hey, we don't need you. You haven't got through college yet.'

Steve Jobs, founder of Apple Computer Inc., on attempts to get Atari and Hewlett-Packard interested in his and Steve Wozniak's personal computer

In a few minutes a computer can
make a mistake so great that it would take
many men many months to equal it.

Merle Meacham

640K ought to be enough for anybody.

Bill Gates, 1981

First Law of Systems Planning:
Anything that can be changed will be changed
until there is no time left to change anything.

Computer salesman: This computer is designed
to cut your workload by fifty per cent.
Employee: Hey, great! I'll take two.

Computing power increases as the square of the cost. If you want to do it twice as cheaply, you have to do it four times as fast.

Anonymous

A first-grade teacher was overseeing her students as they experimented with their desk computers. One boy sat staring at the screen, unsure how to get the computer going. The teacher walked over and read what was on the screen. In her most reassuring voice, she said, 'That computer wants to know what your name is.' Then she walked over to the next child. The boy leaned forward and whispered, 'My name is David.'

Joe Claro, ***The Random House Book of Jokes***

FORE
GOLF TOUR
GOLF TOUR

Bo

The computer is down; if our world needs an epitaph, and it may, could there be a better?

*Bernard Levin, **A Walk Up Fifth Avenue***

Computers are definitely more clever than humans. When's the last time six computers got together to form a committee.

Anonymous

'Have you had a busy day at the office?' asked a young woman to her husband when he returned home late.

'Terrible,' he said. 'The computers went down in the middle of the afternoon and we had to think.'

Employer: Our programmer is
a biblical programmer.
Employee: What's that?
Employer: She believes in filing things according to the Biblical proverb: 'Seek and ye shall find ...'

If operating systems were beer:

VMS Beer: Requires minimal user interaction, except for popping the top and sipping. However cans have been known on occasion to explode, or contain extremely un-beer-like contents. Best drunk in high pressure development environments. When you call the manufacturer for the list of ingredients, you're told that is proprietary and referred to an unknown listing in the manuals published by the FDA. Rumours are that this was once listed in the Physicians' Desk Reference as a tranquillizer, but no one can claim to have actually seen it.

To the tune of 'The Twelve Days of Christmas':
(last stanza)
With the twelfth bug of Christmas,
my manager said to me ...

1. Tell them it's a feature
2. Say it's not supported
3. Change the documentation
4. Blame it on the hardware
5. Find a way around it
6. Say they need an upgrade
7. Reinstall the software
8. Ask for a dump
9. Run with the debugger
10. Try to reproduce it
11. Ask them how they did it
12. See if they can do it again

Employer: How good are your wp skills?
Secretary: Well, the keying-in isn't so great – but I can erase eighty words per minute!

The computer is an inadequate substitute for human intelligence, but then so are a lot of executives.

Anonymous

The world's first full computerized airliner was ready for its maiden flight without pilots or crew. The plane taxied to the loading area automatically, its doors opened automatically. The passengers boarded the plane and took their seats.

The seats retreated automatically, the doors closed, and the airplane taxied towards the runway.

'Good afternoon, ladies and gentlemen,' a voice intoned. 'Welcome to the debut of the world's first fully computerized airliner. Everything on this aircraft is run electronically. Just sit back and relax. Nothing can go wrong ... nothing can go wrong ... nothing can go wrong ...'

Joe Claro, ***The Random House Book of Jokes***

Acknowledgements:

The Publishers wish to thank everyone who gave permission to reproduce the quotes in this book. Every effort has been made to contact the copyright holders, but in the event that an oversight has occurred, the publishers would be delighted to rectify any omissions in future editions of this book. Grateful thanks for submissions by Eric Theil and his team at Quark, transmitted by Compuserve; *The Random House Book of Jokes and Anecdotes*, Joe Claro, reprinted courtesy of Random House Inc., *Murphy's Law*, Arthur Bloch, reprinted by permission of Methuen London; *Sunday Times*, reprinted courtesy of Times Newspapers Limited.